GODDESS PAGES:

Honey, Full Moons and Daggers

Shepsa

authorHOUSE®

AuthorHouse™
1663 Liberty Drive
Bloomington, IN 47403
www.authorhouse.com
Phone: 1-800-839-8640

Photos: Vanessa D. Woods
Cover Design: Rico Frederick Web: RicoFDK.com

Published by AuthorHouse   04/02/2012

ISBN: 978-1-4685-7733-4 (sc)
ISBN: 978-1-4685-7727-3 (hc)
ISBN: 978-1-4685-7732-7 (e)

Library of Congress Control Number: 2012906013

CONTENTS

Dedication vii

Acknowledgements ix

Part One: Honey, The Love Goddess

Letter to My Man (for tonight) 1

The Massage 4

Down in the Delta 6

Inspired 8

Conjure Man 9

For Love 11

Sweat Dance 12

I AM Goddess 15

Food of the Gods 18

Make Me an Orgasm 20

Sacred Sex 23

desire 28

My LOVE 30

Double Entendre 34

Part Two: Full Moons, The Mother Goddess

Generations 41

To Mother 45

For Us 48

Statue 50

Friday Nite Blues 54

Supernatural 56

This Boy 58

Single Mothers 60

On Leaving 63

Part Three: Daggers, The War Goddess

BAD I AM 69

Erzulie Dantor 73

Troy 74

I Wanna Love You Without White People 76

My World View 79

slaveship 80

Soldier 82

For Saartje 84

Daughter of Mars 87

sara jane 90

Crazy Bitch 94

DEDICATION

To the Goddess within us all, may She guide you to birth your deepest truth. To my mothers, grandmothers and all women who have bled their dreams onto the roadmap of humanity. It is because of them we live.

ACKNOWLEDGEMENTS

I give thanks to every single teacher I ever had from Anderson Elementary school, through the halls of NYU, to my son Maa Kheperab. I also give a special thanks to every spiritual teacher and institution I have ever been a part of. Every single experience has made these poems possible. Special thanks to Ainsley Burrows for assistance with editing and being a lighthouse during this process. Shout out to Kenya K. Stevens and the whole JujuMama family for creating a process by which this baby could be born. Lastly, Modupe to my Ancestors, empower me to live up to my name.

INTRODUCTION

Welcome to the Goddess Pages where I travel between three worlds, three personas but all one woman, all me, all Goddess. This book has been in embryo for over five years. For over five years I have sat in labor, many times thinking I had suffered a miscarriage, but here is my newborn baby. Allow my words to mix with yours; the stories, insights, clichés to find a space within your memory. This is not just about poetry, this is a journey. Over the past year I have reconnected to my voice. Like many people in general, women in particular, I had closed off my truth after having a child and "settling" down. I stuffed all my passion and creativity away in exchange for stability and security. But the artist within has resurged, rocketing from the depths of my being.

For the last decade, I have explored ancient traditions that have existed since time was born and in this journey, I have made connections with the feminine aspect of the Divine; recognizing Her presence and power within me and without. You do not have to be a believer in this to enjoy my poetry. You can look at your mother, your sister, your wife and yourself to see the power of the Goddess. Listen to Nina Simone sing or watch Josephine Baker dance. Shoot, look at an Erykah Badu video and witness the power of being connected to feminine essence, power and beauty . . .

So this book is divided into three sections representing the three faces of my Goddess. *Part One: Honey, The Love Goddess* features poems dealing in themes of love, attraction, sex and sensuality. *Part Two: Full Moons, The Mother Goddess* deals with themes of womanhood, motherhood, and my emotional underworld. *Part Three: Daggers, The Warrior Goddess* delves into themes of justice, racism and social change.

So yes, I am all of these things. Not just warrior, not just mother and not just lover. I am warrior, mother and lover. I walk the spaces in between these identities too but this is a good place to start. In one moment, I could be soothing my son who just got hurt from his boo-boo, then I might desire to throw a Molotov cocktail at the police for shooting another innocent Black man. Later that night, I might desire to make passionate, scratching-up-the-back-love to my mate. Really, the undercurrent of the faces of all these Goddesses is Love. Hope of a better, just world love. Nurturing and healing blissful love.

—Shepsa

PART ONE: HONEY

The Love Goddess

~⁓

LETTER TO MY MAN
(FOR TONIGHT)

I am thinking of you

letting you in

Your words copulating

my thoughts speaking

to me of healing

our tribe in East Flatbush

with herbs grown under the sun

and moon of Mexico

ripened from squatting in moist

virgin forests

wet with potency

My medicine man

speaking a language

that vibrates on frequencies

ears cannot hear

Shooting out God-rays,

your mouth is the sun

rotate it around the equator

of my hips

This earth your inheritance

your hands map my topography

plant your fingers in the valleys

the sticky rivers of my geography

Yesssssssssssss . . . .

I'll unravel for you tonight

your eyes whisper

you need a healing

I've got new medicines

for you to uncover

Rose quartz and peacock feathers

Sade and sandalwood

burning

Anoint my chakras

with the blessing of your tongue

from crown to root

Let's massage new recollections

into each other's flesh

hidden histories

past lives

loving me under palm trees in Ghana

Pricked palms on cotton thorns in Georgia

In another life we made

love and Revolution

naked under black leather

and berets we fucked

for freedom

So tonight, your body is

a temple of the familiar

My kisses are prayers dancing

across the sanctuary of your chest

Your arms cocoon me

balancing my feminine

A magic wand pulsating

inside my walls rhythmically

You are a thunder

god between my thighs

I am a honey river for you

to swim in

You be butterfly soft

black panther rough

My hips make figure eights

around your tip

as I ride you into infinity

Watching our orgasm explode

in each other's eyes

our love spell echoes

into eternity

The Massage

I need someone to dig in

and loose these knots

Burrow deep

inside flesh and muscle

hard and soft

fast and slow

fresh blood to break up

the tension and stiffness

Lay me out

till I am a limp noodle

a body without bones

Pry me open

till I gush,

screaming

a steamy river

I need someone to dig in

and loose these knots

Pound a new rhythm

into these tendons

pulse and vibrate

sound and silence

Awaken a beat

~Shepsa~

send me spinning

Lay flat the old patterns

till I am a sea

of call and response

A song

without breaks and blues

Stretch me open

till I roar

singing

a sweet volcano

Down in the Delta

this old blues

is squeezing blackberry juice

out my soul

a slow grind on top

of a piano

laid out on the backseat

of a Cadillac

my legs peacock spread

over pink flamingo suede

fingernails piercing vinyl cushions

blue grass bending into

angular breaths and acappella screams

vintage sex fuck me

down to Mississippi delta

sugar shacks and smoke houses

archie moore knockout

in the third round at sunrise

i'd make flapjacks

and homefries for you

come skittering back

for a rematch

distorted

watermelon wet

sweet potato thighs

squeezing you into blue notes

twisted sideways

nasty sharecropper sweat

dripping hoochie coochie baptisms

sipping moonshine from your lips

i'd sin on sunday

ass backwards

spinning eight tracks

on the altar

of you

Inspired

it's been a long time
since
i felt inspired
maybe while traveling
Mt. Kilimanjaro
in Kenya
but you inspire me
till I am giggling inside
like a coy
geisha girl
till my thoughts
are a mosh pit
of ecstatic fans
wishing for you
to crowd surf on their heads
i think you are Joplin
or Hendrix
or Baldwin
call me Zora
or Josephine
or Nina
let's make
a Renaissance . . .

Conjure Man

Tie me in your mojo bag

You don't need no bones

or crushed herbs

calling spirits

I will bring the

vodou down

Got a spell

dripping down my back

Just missing your candle

Every pore begging

for your midnight chant

Sing in my lap

a drum beat rolling

rivers inside my thighs

I could climb you

ride all the way to Afrika

Don't disobey your ancestors

They have knit us together

Don't you know

what Shepsa means?

When you enter me

I feel you down

to your lineage

This is anything but simple

I would heal

all your generations

Have your descendants

pouring libations to me

We be wildseed

birthing a nation of seers

Children of Sirius

walking milky ways

Constellations

written on our face

Kiss me

and feel our power

The pulse of Venus

bleeding light years

of love

For Love

Love is
a disobedient child
that does not suffer rules
caught with its hands
in the cookie jar
suckling sweets
in spite the risk
of cavities
If Love was a hurricane,
its' name would be
Katrina
Bursting levees
meant to contain its power,
drowning
all those unprepared
the forsaken
swallowed
in its flood
If my Love had a name,
it would be Bandit
stealing me
kicking
and screaming
over to you . . .

Sweat Dance

11 am
i come in
dance the sweat
off from you
under brooklyn pipe water
my choice would be
to let it stain
like your thrust
does my memories
we backstroke
on white sheets
doggy paddle
inside glasses of bacardi
if I chained you
to my thighs
would you call me
an overseer?
could we be
a love-slaveship?
i promise
i'd emancipate you
at the end

of this lifetime

maybe you could

reincarnate as

my clit

or I could be the pink

that hugs

your tongue

i hunger for you

like sky

hungers blue

i want you

in my bloodstream

the eye of your storm

inside my cells

come

rain fluorescent pearls

on my chest

i'll wear you

like a belt

this is heroine

i am a poppy seed addict

or maybe

rose quartz flavored hookah

swallowing eight balls of you . . . .

my hands

start to shake

as I come down

from_our sweat dance

you uncork me

it is always new years eve

dick clark

is finally dead

and my whole body

is lit

like times square

I AM GODDESS

If you could feel
the thunder
between my thighs
it would give you whip lash
Hit you so fast
you'd be cross-eyed
My body a boom of healing
sliding up your spine
Kundalini energy
connecting me
to you,
so deep you might get confused
and think it's about you
But it ain't!
I've been doing this
for centuries
Way back
in the days of the Goddess,
My Isis was so sick
I could create immaculately,
give birth to a God
from the seed of my dead king

Divine energy
shooting
through my body,
I be Shakti
The temple's my yoni,
fuck a new universe
through me
I AM the big bang!
My orgasm gave birth
to the galaxy
What do they call me?
They call me sweet thing . . . .
I bet the neighbors
know my name
The planets
know my name
Call me Venus
Bare breasted,
snake charmer
cat eye enchantress
Tantra priestess
Come see me
for your healing
I put those sexually commodified
Black woman stereotypes
to rest,
taste the sugar

dripping from my breast

Enter the river of my wetness

Come and fill me

with your yang,

warrior king

do your thang

Make me call you Shango

I'll be your Oshun

from Oshogbo,

enchanting you

with my sweet honey dance

Daughter of the moon

Call me Kali

I hail from the land

of the Black Goddesses,

We be twizzler twirled in space,

ejaculating stars,

Leave you spellbound

with my sex magic

I speak my vodou clearly

Love you down

Lay you out

Kill you

with my sex therapy!

Food of the Gods

my peach is humming honey

sticky drip

across purple lips

pushing mango juice

down cinnamon thighs

you should taste me

lick me into anguish

your soft suckling

has me sailing

i'm drunk

off your tongue

oh Loverman

hear me scat some Ella

up the scales of my spine

hit my blue note

make me scream

in harmony

off pitch

get tangled inside me

let me rollercoaster you

i wanna talk to angels

they envy us

there is some good

in the flesh

this moment,

our immortality

i tasted the glyphs

on your brown obelisk

drank the creamy sacred

thread me into your memory

i want to live forever

like the Titans

you can be black Orpheus

spitting poetry

into the carnival

of my clit

sing me into calypso

i'll wine you down to dub

no words

only swallowed rhythms

echoing till we

oracle

a new day

Make Me an Orgasm . . . .

Imagine
in the beginning was darkness
spread thick like molasses
Goddess breathed
upon it and said,
Right now it's only me
lonely up here by myself
She split in half
gave birth to God
Together they said,
Hey let Us make We a world
She became a snake
and she hid herself
inside of him
in the cliff of his spine
sent a signal to his right brain
saying, *Make me come*
He gyrated till she cobraed
could feel her
sitting on the throne of his head
that glowed violet
then white

Spiraled herself around him
her sepia legs knotting a bow
below his waist
He could feel her
watering
till the air was oceans and rivers
He entered her
like a volcano rising
pumping her with the fire
needed to birth creation
Each stroke he gave her
deposited minerals
in the milky way
between her legs
Pleased her for 100,000 light years
digging his hydrogen
inside her nucleus
till they were swirling
protons and electrons
going harder faster
in and out
They could feel
the blocks of the universe
building
building
building
He said are you ready?
She said yes

They locked eyes,
arms, lips,
hips and exploded
at a billion degrees
creating time
Her clit beat like a drum
till she squirted
matter
and light
and darkness
planets, suns and moons
He throbbed
like a jack hammer
Ejaculated
the 7 seas
vegetation
creatures that move
upon the ground
and swim in air
She released
He penetrated
Till the galaxy was pregnant
with humanity
Birthed from the divine
who swam from a celestial seed
Fueled by orgasms
In the beginning . . . .

SACRED SEX

I wanna sex you

I wanna sacred you

I need a miracle

There has been

 a drought this season

making my Nile Valley thirsty

Come show me

when u were king

Have u ever fucked

a Goddess?

I'd tattoo my chants

across your tongue

Worship me

in Ebonics and Sanskrit

Call me your baby mama

Lakshmi

Standing on a lotus flower

doing a striptease

Downward facing dog,

upward facing dog

Come plank me

I'll be your yogi

Bring me offerings

mangoes, whips and honey

tantra manuals,

handcuffs and cherries

Lay me down on your altar

echo prayers

inside the temple

of my pussy

Crown my yoni the holiest of holies

Lighting bolt me

I wanna feel your super bass

thundering

inside me

Make me quiver out an

oh-oh-ohhhhhh-ohhhmmmmm . . . .

My sex is sacred

I'm somewhere between

pole dancer and priestess

stripper and sorceress

porno and prophetess

Come down Moses

and part my seas

Plant your staff

inside my sticky waters

you descendant of Kush

I'm looking for a God

Come speak in tongues

to my burning bush

while I tempt you

with my ten commandments

Thou shalt lick me

Thou shalt kiss me

Thou shalt covet me

Thou shalt love me

Thou shalt not have

any strange Goddess

before me

Shout my name,

bullets in your veins with ecstasy

Remember Tantra Tuesday,

keep it holy

Honor me and I will feed you ginseng

so that your nights

may last longer

Carve images of my hips

worship me beside rivers

You shall never forget

I always come first . . .

I'll be your promised land

The secrets encoded

in the spine of the universe

I wanna go blind

seeing only the chocolate

woven into your flesh

Call me Godiva

go diva

god diva

dancing the holy ghost

in a g string

It's a revival

convert you into a

punany Pentecostal

A dominatrix disciple

Come experience my

laying on of hands

get delivered

I want your sin

Have you hemorrhaging

hallelujahs

baptized in deep stroke sweat

Make you my apostle

ministering teachings

from the g-spot gospel

Witnessing words whispered

between the thighs

of my bible

I wanna initiate you

Turn you into a practitioner

of my vodou

You can stick pin me

till I gush

holy waters

coochie covenants

cunnilingus communions

Eat this

of my body and remember me

Orgasm creamy crucifixions

throbbing resurrections

A second coming

We can come again . . . .

Cause my sex

is so sacred

My sin is so perfect

I have Jesus wishing

he never died

a virgin

DESIRE

i would be a telegraph

from the taj mahal

singing love letters

in your dreams

why do you play with me

like this?

i've seen you before . . . .

a Masai blazing the savannah

scorching inheritance

and royalty

i wanted you then

like the farmer's wife wants the cock

to crow

to midwife a new day

i want you now

in my earth's core

touch this lava

a pathology of desire

would turn Brooklyn

into ash

we could stand

in the ruins

statue ourselves

be a temple of arms and legs

my thighs would

suck you

into pools of magic

i could purify you

you know this

and that's why

you stay

away . . .

MY LOVE

My love be

the praise songs

of shamans

chanting over herbs

as ancient as pyramids

to awaken

their celestial blueprints

to heal the heart of man

My love be

the flipped switch

that unleashes coiled serpents

as dangerous as acid

that electrifies the brain

My love is

a rare and sacred orchid

watered

by the tears of a child

made breathless

by its' beauty

My love be

Marvin and Tammi

You're all I need to get by . . . .

Method Man and Mary

I got a love jones

for your body and your skin tone . . .

glyphed on project walls

My love be

as old as time

as new as time

as future as time

Circular like the hips of Jupiter

Sharp and bludgeoning

like the horns of Taurus

governed by Venus

A raging bull

unleashed

and undulated

by Jamaican girls

in dutty whine contests

My love be

sashaying

down Eastern Parkway

in ostrich feathers

and sequins

to soca

Throwing kisses

to brown people

flicking colorful flags
from their hands
like the tongue of a cobra

My love be
after birth bloody and thick
Nutrient rich
Omega 8's
and antioxidants
Healthy like
protein shakes
and vitamin c supplements
My love be
Khufu's pyramid huge and perfect
Tracking solstices,
communicating with stars
and planets

My love would 9-11 you
Imploding
and disintegrating
the tall towers of your ego
Leaving you
at ground zero
with a handful of ashes
and memories

My love be

laffy taffy sweet and sticky

chocolate Sunday

hershey kiss me

Sugar daddy,

milky way blast me

Come give me

your good and plenty

My kit kat,

your butterfinger

Caramel cream me

Make me remember

My love . . . .

Let us

merge

like sun setting

into dusk

naked

as the sea

Double Entendre

I could stretch out
inside of you
like Miles Davis's
kind of blue
Blanket myself
under your horns
Each word a track
the conversation an lp
pushed on repeat
in my mind . . . .

Let's not talk
about the dance
I can testify
there is only One
With you
I am so myself
that "I" is dispersed
and the frame of me
is smashed
against the walls

of the universe

till I am but a vapor

whose only delight

is to be

inhaled

by you . . . .

I wonder

who told you

to move inside

my mind

I see you couched

on my cerebrum

Feet resting on my cerebellum

till I am a dangling dichotomy

of body mind separation

washing the dishes

cooking the dinner

checking the email

while my thoughts

are somewhere

chain ganged to you . . .

I'd like to unshackle you

from my cerebral cortexes

We can keep the handcuffs

I'd place you under house arrest

sentence you

to mandatory minimums

of three hours hard labor

inside

my diamond mines

till you starburst

Come snake yourself

in my DNA

till we double helix

and spiral out

a new creation

Let's name her

double entendre

We will speak

with forked tongues

Kiss me

till I bleed your name

Each letter a moan

that earthquakes

out my mouth

May our tremors

tip the richter scale

till you are tsunamied

send your soldier

to go skinny dipping

deep inside my trenches

Capture my pussy

as a prisoner of war

I'll offer you

an orgasm

as a ransom

PART TWO: FULL MOONS

The Mother Goddess

GENERATIONS

I. Souf

I come from southern

baptist women

bred on sunday dinners

and bootleg liquor

church picnics in Norf Carolina

slow grinds to

Muddy Waters in jukes,

Jezebel women

butterflied into evangelists

giving baptisms in cherokee rivers

big legs baking in high heel shoes

thundering dirt roads

sensitive to sex

and men with oak tree backs

who dance spider kisses

across their neck

black widow

out of wedlock women

swaddling babies in psalms

spanking them with revelations

sweating watermelon juice

into picnic baskets

pouring negro hymns

into collard greens

dressed in white

jingling tambourines

spilling the spirits of Pentecost

slain with silence, women

threading midnights together

to find peace

Carolina Ibo women

with scarlet eyes

etching stars into the night

with the tears of a panther

My belly is filled

with their screams

My belly is filled

with their songs

II. Norf

I come from

Norf Philly women

bread on dirt and danger

street fights in classrooms

tongue tussles

under full moons

6 brothers

5 sisters

4 different fathers

2 bedroom apartment women

concrete jungle amazonians

kicking ass

circling street lights

in cigarette smoke

spearing rapists

with survivor

in their eyes

daughters of a domestic worker

stitching ragdolls from table cloths

song-less soprano women

breathing amazing grace

into stairwells

poor but hip women

spitting curses

like seeds

sweet sex smells

perfuming the air of rent parties

gifting children to chaos

to birth the possibility

of tomorrows

my back don't break women

working till blood

runs from their eyes

and spells pour

from their fingers

North Philly Nubian women

with sangria mouths

french kissing the night

with the tongue of a lioness

My bones are heavy

with their dance

My bones are heavy

with their daggers

To Mother

Womb
becomes magical pot
of vertebrae, soul and cells
ancestral embryo
ciphering thoughts,
Breathe for me
heartbeat for me
eat and drink for me
later, bleed for me
Let me make you fat
ache your back
Rip you open
Stretch your skin
till it is a road map
of bulging highways
and sunken cities
Mommy, your body
a sacrament
without ceremony . . .

No one is breaking bread
and sipping wine for me

I want me a cathedral

Bring me back to my temples

stain glass windows

coffee colored

colossal statues

titties out

belly in bulge

hips and curves

baby on lap

as we nurse a nation

Oh Eve, you were never cursed

We are a garden

of snake dancers

forbidden fruit breaking

morning between our legs

A petaled peach of dynamite

sustaining contractions

that could rupture cities

Our womb a gateway

to Atlantis

Our wet carries the ph balance

of God's breath

Beaming men up

seven layers of heaven

to have them plummet to earth

again

Begging to be reborn

to salute at our shrines

to have our breast milk

fatten their bellies

To have our thighs

swallow their seeds

reincarnation

swimming inside

the sacred of us

Mother.

For Us

We don't want

to be so hard

Us

Black women

we love our children

love our men

love the sweat and tears out of them

Our passion,

a boa constrictor

squeezing the world

When we hurt,

it is a wild fire

a rampage of pain

Face becomes a shield

of twisted lips and rolling eyes

We are rougher

than our men

Our tongue iron spears

but if you could hear

the silver and gold

mined by our laughter

could see the pink ocean

~Shepsa~

blanketing our souls

Massage the red knots

of anger away

You would see Us

a thorned rose

a half dream

a dammed flood

wanting to explode

Combust in love

Bodies full of tension

breaking a song of release

melting into holy

awakened

pure

~

Statue

Mommy,

let me make

a statue of you

it will be

how you never were

soft

Your name will not

be Work Horse

Your name will not

be Mule

I will carve you in jade

you will be called

angel of the womb

The throne of kings

will rest on your head

The moon will dangle

from your neck

Goddesses will embrace you

and shed indigo tears

for the years

you never wet your eyes

Life cut continents of pain

~Shepsa~

in your palms

Empty belly

biting hunger

White girl ragdoll

leftovers

The street gang

that left railroad tracks

across your back

Kidnapped

taken on a train

you could not get off of

Our father

rummaging

through your purse

for loose change

to buy some blow

To blow

the Charlie Parker

blues of his soul

You,

an unbalanced equation

of survival

Perfect right angle of anger

on your hips

at any sign of your daughters

being fresh

Perpendicular punches
intersect your son's chest
for report card F's
Love for you
had always been an injury
Your brother
opened a gate to eternity
pointing a revolver
to his belly
How could you stomach
that by yourself?
Tried to birth a black man
who would not walk
with a noose around his neck
Named him Ronald Jr.
Scottish for wise ruler
34 years later
your only son
attempts to pipe dream
his nightmares away
Your wish was for us
to survive
ghetto landmines
so we would not have to soldier
The pain you've had to shoulder
fatigued you
war until sun bleeds

into night

We were scared of

the detonation of

your tongue

Bring yo ass here!

Stop that crying 'fore I give you

something

to cry about!

You never go about

crying

Mommy,

Let me make

a monument of

Your tears will be

diamonds

You will sit on

a throne of lions

You will wear a crown

of cobras

It will be what you

never were,

Protected.

Loved.

Friday Nite Blues

every friday nite

i get the blues

it is a scripted injury

single mama

playing guitars of lonely

deep south

work songs

ring shouts

moaning down

the corners of my eyes

dancing the juba

on my ribcage

lady day planting

a flower in her hair

like a hypodermic needle

like a smile used

to swallow memories

of hungry kisses

when the blues

was not enough song

to bring harmony

to the soul

howling wolf grinding lighting

from the barrel of his chest

like a train racing to the moon

like a fist squeezing

sugar cane into molasses

when the blues was not enough

dark sweet

to bring joy to the soul

every friday nite

i get the blues

its an aborted orgasm

single mama playing

saxophones of want

harlem jazz

crawling notes

from the corners

of my mouth

my soul smoking its

reefers

SUPERNATURAL

I am supernatural
felling trees with my mouth
Climbing mountains with my breath
Do you see these beads?
Each one is a God
Each one sings a song
Each one has its' own dance
I am Yemaya
wrapped in the shroud of Turin
Some of this cotton
is still specked with blood
Thorn pricked palms
did not forget
the magic of roosters
Machete wielding hands
did not drop their
16 cowrie shells
Always remembered
the importance of cool water
Songs called lightening
and thunder to dance
the night
A people who knew

how to pray the wind
Offerings waking the dead
at cemeteries
Cabildo drumming
causing slave masters
to toss and turn
scared of spirits
who danced the mambo
Mambos who knew how to
dance the spirits
down the axis of the earth
Whip cracking hands
trembling nightmares
of Hougans who carved Kongo
insignias in cornmeal
Astral gateways opening
on enslaved lands
Burning crops
smoking revolution . . .
I am supernatural
walking the voice
of my ancestors
A million Bantu
and Yoruba spirits
whispering recipes
into my daydreams
They speak
the blood
in my veins.

THIS BOY

5 years old

5,000 years young

warrior breaking in Zulu

your soul's imprint

long as the Mississippi

always, always

a rocket of questions

sometimes

you are not looking

for answers

you are practicing thought

a way of bending sound

into subtle critiques

i knew you

when you were

invisible

heard your voice

wafting at the pink

lake in Senegal

your face floated to me

on rose colored waters

your spirit

tracked mine for 7 years

till you crossed to this side

made a home in my womb

i see the man

sitting on the stool

of your soul

he reaches out

and plays the drum

with your baby hands

those that can not see him

fall speechless at your technique

a baby holding his hands

like he was born in Guinea?

like he spent his days

in the grove of Shango

you walk the streets of Bed-Stuy

spinning cartwheels

making the world

sing it's song

you are Imhotep

beatboxing

Sam Cooke's blues

Single Mothers

We swap war stories

like we were Iraq war veterans

who suffered a bad IED

where our hearts

were caught in the detonation

living the rest of our lives

as cardiac amputees

I do not want

to be this tin man

of a woman

There is still a rhythm beating

in this chest

I reject the term survivor

Playgrounds have become

refugee camps for young divorcees

to watch their children climb

their jungle gym dreams

Seeing their babies happy

is a congressional medal of honor

But just settling

for the day to day wins

in the battle of single motherhood

~Shepsa~

is not enough

I often loose to temper tantrums

and daddy's cancelled visits

It is hard

not to let your heart

become a soviet bloc

of strong armed troops

ready to war

against the freedom of man

For Us

parenting is never a choice

an appointment placed on a schedule

subject to last minute changes

Rearranged to a more convenient

time to father

Nature trains mothers quickly

to rise at the first sound of alarm

Newborn cries unhinging eyes

from sleep

as you look over

at the blanketed mass of masculinity

that did not even stir

You realize your body

was booby-trapped

for this

nursing your babies hunger

away . . .

The imbalance of the scales

can leave you cold

But I refuse to become

this reptile of a woman

I will not camouflage myself

with the colors of survival

I am bold enough

to become a flame

Paint me crimson

Tie bells to my ankles

so that the wind

will streak red

and the air will laugh

wherever I walk

I will finger print my future

No cookie cutter war stories

No chain gang love songs

No loose lipped birds flying low

singing of broken dreams

On Leaving...

To be young,

Black and Married

is to be crowned

with milk and honey

I had done the right thing

to be so young

to have a child

How many women my age

were still handing out numbers

in the club

Complaining how that nigga

never called

I spent Friday nights

massaging sore nipples

He was my first you know

I was supposed to be

one and done

Had did everything teacher's pet

since kindergarten

Captain of the debate team

A wall with my face on it

eighty feet high

They called me a Black Madonna
I used to really be into Jesus . . .

Secret is
we never exchanged vows
A commitment without ceremony
Papers pushed through
priestly hands
given the holy seal of a signature
I cannot tell you
the date it was official
It was sometime in October
Everyone around me
had swallowed the watermelon seed
Wearing ankhs around our necks
frying tofu and making veggie steak
I began to see the carpet of my life
rolled out before me
My head stuck inside
a cardboard cut out
of his parents
Me holding baby,
handcuffed to house
Him in blue transit uniform,
eyes red from moving buses
in the graveyard shift
2 years later

10 years later

20 years later

Parts of me

were being buried somewhere

Needed to unearth myself

Wanted to mommy but

not to mummy

Marriage like bandages

constraining my limbs

A corset squeezing

the wings from my lungs

My life is no coffin

My breasts were made to breathe . . .

On leaving . . . .

I did not want to hurt him

I have no Tyler Perry

stories to tell you

of how he beat or cheated on me

No angry Black woman diaries

Happy is not

just for white women

He wanted me to stay for our son

But I left for our son

To create a new mythology

where marriage does not mean bondage

Where love is food for expansion

and passion is fuel for time

Ain't

Never

Been

Easy

Sometimes my son's cries

for daddy

can rip the stars from his eyes

But when they fall

I pluck him one

Place the five points on his chest

Tell him he is a supernova

brighter than 10 billion suns,

Don't ever curve your light

to fit inside

someone else's spectrum

There are no mistakes,

only lessons

I called this on Leaving,

But it is really

on Living.

PART THREE: DAGGERS

The War Goddess

BAD I AM

I fasted for four hundred years
made my way
through the wilderness
following the North Star,
while carrying 100 million
Africans on my head.
The devil tried to tempt me
saying if I let him
William Lynch me
he would give me the kingdom.
I wanted freedom instead,
so I Died.

This ol' Devil
wanted to rule the world,
so he chopped me up
and spread my body around
to fourteen different places
thinking
I could never get myself
back together again.

But out of each piece
grew a Black nation,
and my children
used my body as a compass
to lead them back to Africa
They buried me on Goree Island
where the souls of slaves slept.
On the third day I arose
with my peoples' original name
in my hand
I crowned them,
Mandinka and Akan.
Kush and Kamit.
Then I talked shit
to the devil's face
letting him know how BAD I AM.
"Lookey here devil,
you can never crucify me!
I walk across the sea
watch it part behind me.
'Cross burning sands
made pyramids rise in front of me.
You need to hide
in the cleft of that rock
as I pass through,
My divinity will blind you,

you can only see my tail . . .
need to understand my legacy!
I've fed 5,000 children
with my five breasts
carried them all on my two legs.
All who ate were full
I still have some left over.
I will not whisper it any more
America was built
on my back,
breast milk,
birth and blood
on the seventh day it was good
but I have yet to rest.
Put your hand in my side
you can see where I bled,
the fifty lashes you gave me.
all the years you raped me.
You allowed
our mulatto son Judas
to betray me.
But lookey here devil,
I've come back from the dead
to bind you for a thousand years.
There will be no more
weeping or gnashing of teeth

Hell or slave ships
gunshots or ghettos.
I will ascend to the throne
my ancestors
have prepared for me,
It will be called, BAD I AM
My people will pour libation
in remembrance of me.

Erzulie Dantor

I will bathe you

in rainbow flower petals

and fire

Dress me in blue taffeta

and daggers

Sing my hails

Sing my silence

It was me you called

in the mountains

commanding troops

of the dead

I led you to freedom

on the back of a black pig

You are hungry

come to me

You are dark

come to me

You are woman with child

come to me

I will be a sharpened blade

flashing your protection

Pierced hearts

that cry blood tears

TROY

9/21/11
if they could see my spirit
it would be hovering
over prison labyrinths
collecting the souls
of innocent men
lynched on Georgia trees
injection tables
i would swarm
from rows of cells
to rows of cotton
leading an invisible army
whose wrist bled
from the chew of shackles,
whose backs curved with
the cargo of chains
i'd unhinge the screams
of cree and cherokees
trapped in swamps
our song would blast
their barbed wire
and cinder blocks

~Shepsa~

speaking the tongue

of a hurricane

hornets would nest the eyes

of God's impostors

our court would be supreme

it would be

Just Us

Brothas and Sistas

with heads trapped

in the mouth of a lion

we'd reverse it

and become the Sphinx

their ashes would be sand

under our feet . . .

I WANNA LOVE YOU WITHOUT WHITE PEOPLE

I wanna love you

without white people

without a noose around your neck

without hands that clutch

and claw your manhood

Front page it beast

Jail it savage

I wanna love you

in sparkling water fountains

of COLORED ONLY

In lunch counters and empty

Alabama water hoses

I wanna Frantz Fanon

love your Black skin

peeling away it's white mask

I would blend and serenade

the dogged

double consciousness of you

I wanna love your face

in Pharaohs

in the Sphinx

~Shepsa~

Big nose carved

from the bedrock of Giza

Skin bronzed in Benin

Free of Napoleons

and Conquistadors

I wanna love you without fear

of beasts in blue

making target practice

of your body

Nightmares of wallets

swimming in pools

of bullets and blood

I wanna love you

into Nat Turner rebellions

and machetes

Malcolm swinging Emmett Till's revenge

Let me take away

the slave ships sailing

middle passages in your eyes

I can still hear their screams

from the hold when I hold you

I wanna love you into Shaka Zulu

with an army of Moors

riding white horses into the capital

on election day

I wanna love you

without adam and eve

birthing you in black sin

so that you need a white man

to come save you

I would wordship you

into godhood

Erect frescos of you in metaphor

You be candles

and confessional booths for me

Orunmila and Tehuti

I wanna love you

into a sea of baby soft

made salty by my tears

smoothing the tarred and feathered

pages of our history

I wanna love you

I want to love

and feel you

Black

Black

and free . . .

My World View

The world is a john,
white supremacy is a whore
spreading its disease
venereally.
The world is the raped,
white supremacy is the rapist,
holding open the legs
of every country.

SLAVESHIP

metal dragon

singing the hymn of

electrical fetishes

black bodies

pressed together

in a hurry

a cage of limbs

mechanical doors

opening like tombs

more bodies spilling in

clawing for space

something to hold onto

to wrench their hope around

to curve the weight of dead ends

freedom on a leash

paid for with sit-ins and water hoses

bought with boycotts and swollen feet

neo-negroes chained with uncertainty

lullabied to sleep

with the comfort of wants

with the want of comfort

forgotten North Stars

no crazy Black ladies

spinning revolvers

to lead the way

we travel on railroads

built underground

to good masters

cracking pension whips

to the beat

of corporate plantations

someone sing us a spiritual

give us a coded message

through our ipods

help us to feel our hearts

pulsing for emancipation

drumming for a new day

Soldier

you said, freedom

they said, shoulder a musket

bail out your body

with the liberation

of your blood

where should I go?

you asked

they answered

Virginia

Korea

Germany

Vietnam

Iraq

Los Angeles

everywhere you went

they searched for the tail

between your legs

rippled their face

with confusion

whoever heard

of fighting the enemy

of the enemy

to still be seen

as an enemy

homeland?

every time

you fought

your mouth would foam

red, white and blue

at most they scripted you

a B list

guest star of history

they ate their own

for growing their hair long

beat them down in brixton

tuskegee symbolizes

booker t.

airmen

and syphilis

they will commend you

and bury you

with a single breath

soldier

fight your war

but don't be

a cog in their machine

be the rapid dog

whose teeth

breaks the wind in

it's wheels

For Saartje

Went to South Africa
in search of the bones
of Saartje Baartman
I heard they were buried
in the sands of women's faces
from Capetown
to Brooklyn
They were closeted skeletons
of touched shame
falling from their mouths
21st century Hottentots
bending over
the echo of cackles and cat calls
from piccadilly circus
19th century exhibition of
Black Venus
French and Brits tripping
over their fear of black ass
Filled with lust and spectacle
Needed to cage
and finger her vagina
into medical textbooks

While double talking her as

Beautiful

Savage

African

Booty scratcher

Goddess of love

and dissection

Boiled her bones

Pickled her brain

Museumed her

violation and trauma

for over a century

I still hear

Saartje's walk

bleeding in the voices of women

They speak of their

brutalized softness

of the hunger to be protected

the guilt of being sexy

Of liking feathers and sequins

the roundness of their ass

They have held scalpels

to our wombs

Carved them and served them

on plates of rape fantasies

No one will ever fuck you like a black woman

I took her in the bushes she asked for it
Those nigger women are beasts for sex you know
These people of tea and crumpets
fed her their civilization
of prostitution and syphilis
for the love of science
and necrophilia
Took me 28 years
to find the magic in my womb
Embrace the curve of my hips
Worship the liquid dynamite
dripping from my Venus
Stitch the wounds
gaping from 400 years
of rape and dissections . . .
I went to South Africa
searching
for the bones
of Saartje Baartman
I found them
blocking the air
in my throat . . .

DAUGHTER OF MARS

I'm a star ruled by a God
I'm a God ruled by a star
that's ruled by a God
Call me daughter of Mars
I'm war
Purple lightening bolts
painted on my chest
Dressed in red flames
with the head of a lioness
Lapping up blood in battlefields
call me daughter of Saturn
swallowing black holes of time
I birth babies only to eat them
and earth them again
I vibrate inside desert cactuses,
Dressed in indigo skin
Creator of chaos
Dancing the wind
Samba inside cremation grounds
drinking the wine
of decapitated men

Twinkling rings of razor blades

a necklace of swords

A dagger for a tongue

a pitbull for a jaw

Saartje Baartman's revenge

Sally Hemming's emancipation

stomping powdered wig men

Circus them

in front of a congress of whores

Place Jefferson inside a corset

auction him off to his children

copyright his last breath

Daughter of Ra

shooting Harriet's revolver

Freer of slaves

Midnight mother

Matrix spinning black

widow webs

in my womb

Black like the new moon

Darkness like a tomb

Medusa crush rapists

Between the boulders

of my thighs

Miscarriage them with my eyes

I arrive

Bringing powers

the North, South

East and the West

Don't fuck with the Goddess

Got a baby on my breast

and fifty skulls

around my neck

SARA JANE

born with jim crow's tears

in your mouth

tawny hands reaching

for a gravy bowl

of blue eyes

you would spit out

your blackness

put your grandmother

in the closet

strip your flesh

to the bone

hurt too much

to see your mother

collect the dust

from white folks footsteps

pour their dreams

from coffee cups

heard too many

aunties and mammies

rattle the sky

you were just right
half past octoroon
would not enter
from the kitchen
could get by
with skin creamed
with a pinch
of butterscotch
wanted to dance
at Moulin Rouge
for men who jingle
pocket watches
and adultery
pushed your mother
head first
into the cemetery
with a coffin full
of broken hearts

mother knew
it was not all your fault
she felt her tongue tear
every time she had to
choke, yes Ms. Laura
spent her whole life
stitching their solutions

sewed her magic quilts
into their conversations
they would skip off
beaming teeth
blonde hair bouncing
like poodles
your mama knew
you would try
to pirate their laughter
bootleg their sunshine
but never thought
you would curse her
into tar baby
into backdoors
you would climb
into whiteness
on the footstool
of her back

sara jane
your mother died
umbilical cord
strangling her neck
she was blue
with misery
her casket was covered

with white flowers

your voice streaking

trumpets,

"I killed my mother!

I killed my mother!"

and for the first time,

you reached out

for a handful of

blackness to hold

but could

not

CRAZY BITCH

I be this crazy bitch
forking curses
off my tongue
Don't you dare molest my shadow
Don't you dare trigger my gun
I rock porcupine skin
with elephant tusks
bleeding brown like rust
I gust through
blowing black storms of dust
A screaming symphony of ugly
Beethoven you to deaf
A minstrel show of mammy
defecating on the progress
of the talented tenth
Ig'nant
tap dancing subways
begging for
loose change
The rain
turning your slicked back
relaxer into Afrikan puffs

Bone in my noose

fat, black and savage

Witch doctor

weaving Macbethian spells

of dark magic

I'll fetish you

wear your voice like a habit

One night stand turned baby mama

freezing all your assets

A concert of shame

you wanna bury my violins

I'm sitting here

bursting strings

playing a rampage of revenge

Grandmother of history

singing your obituary

like a banshee

Napoleon stone cold liars

you all come from me

From puerto ricans to sicilians

dominicans to dravidians

My bloodline be

nyabinghi dreadlock thick

Crazy Afrikan bitch

Nina Simone casting spells on you

with mojo milk from my tits

Menstrual blood magic tricks

Nappy haired pickaninny

chomping watermelon at picnics

This here mumbo jumbo

be foo-foo and gumbo

Collard greens and pig feet

at the white house

mumbling, *Nigga*

why you faking tone deaf?

Mahalia Jackson weep

a wail from your chest

MJ cultural cardiac arrest

Dirty hoodoo and voodoo

Afrikan booty scratcher

blessed

Mamase mamasa mamakossa

you to death

Call this hymn

of the crazy bitch

Gonna spit till my lips split

Cause I'm singing parts of you

they got you humming

to forget

ABOUT THE AUTHOR

Shepsa is a writer, mother, actress, teacher and juju woman. Born and raised in Philadelphia where her artistic career began, she won numerous awards for her writing at a young age including Presidential Scholar in the Arts, and First Place winner in the Philadelphia Young Playwrights contest. Her face can also be seen as the largest figure in the famous Common Threads mural, which she posed for while attending Creative and Performing Arts high school in Philadelphia. She holds a B.F.A. with honors in Drama from New York University, where she also double majored in Africana Studies. After spending five years devoted to motherhood and spiritual studies, Shepsa has reemerged as an artist and potent voice for young women. *Goddess Pages* is an outpouring of all the "selves" that have emerged in her over the years. She is a student and initiate of several traditional African religions and eastern philosophies. She is a certified i2Tantra practitioner with JujuMama LLC and an awesome teacher. Currently, she teaches theatre to public school students in Brooklyn, NY where she lives with her son.

To stay updated and connected to her work, please visit ladyshepsa.com.

For booking information, contact ladyshepsa@gmail.com.